Saskia Gwinn   Vasilisa Romanenko

Secret Stories of Nature

A Field Guide to Uncover
Our Planet's Past

"All around you, nature is guarding the tales of
the things we know not... bubbling with stories
from a land time forgot."

WIDE EYED EDITIONS

CONTENTS

Secrets of the Sea　　4

Secrets of the Ice　　10

Secrets of the Forest　　16

Secrets of the Jungle　　22

Secrets of the Mountains　　28

Secrets of the Sky　　34

Secrets of the Night　　40

Secrets Underfoot　　46

Searching for Secrets　　52

Finding Earth's Secrets　　58

Protecting Earth's Secrets　　60

Glossary　　62

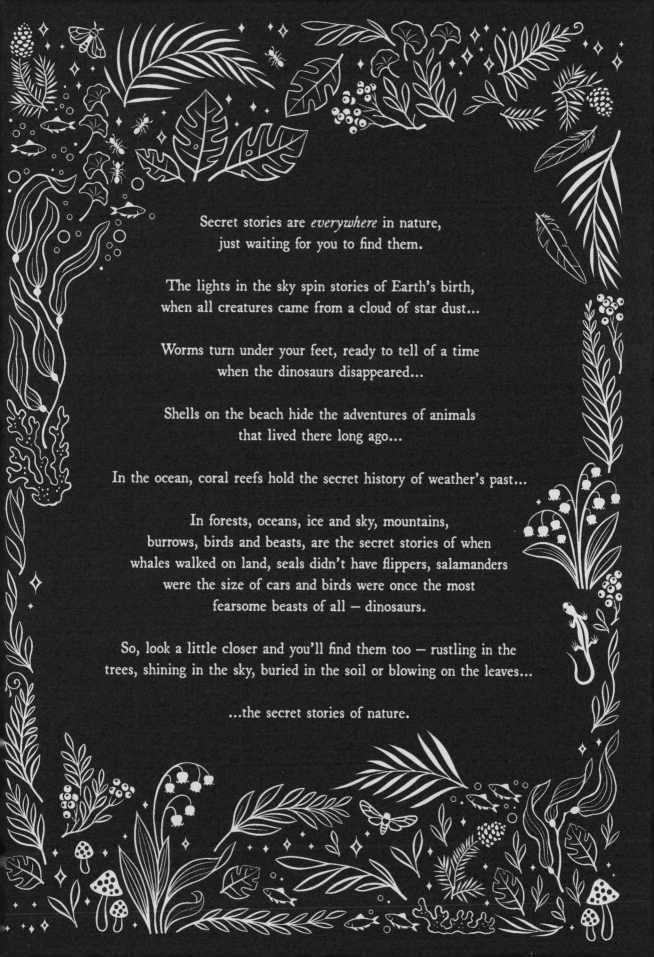

Secret stories are *everywhere* in nature,
just waiting for you to find them.

The lights in the sky spin stories of Earth's birth,
when all creatures came from a cloud of star dust...

Worms turn under your feet, ready to tell of a time
when the dinosaurs disappeared...

Shells on the beach hide the adventures of animals
that lived there long ago...

In the ocean, coral reefs hold the secret history of weather's past...

In forests, oceans, ice and sky, mountains,
burrows, birds and beasts, are the secret stories of when
whales walked on land, seals didn't have flippers, salamanders
were the size of cars and birds were once the most
fearsome beasts of all — dinosaurs.

So, look a little closer and you'll find them too — rustling in the
trees, shining in the sky, buried in the soil or blowing on the leaves...

...the secret stories of nature.

SECRETS OF THE SEA

Our beautiful seas and oceans teem with creatures big and small that keep Earth rich with life. Spectacular starfish move their tiny feet from rock to rock, jaw-dropping jellyfish light up the dark and swift sharks snap up their prey. But this watery world is also an incredible underwater museum, and the creatures that live here hold the keys to unlocking its secret stories. Beneath the waves lie the fossil remains of ancient creatures and colourful coral reefs that can tell of Earth's past climate. Many secrets have been uncovered here, but there is still much to explore...

(1)

(2)

(1) Starfish

Starfish use their arms to move around their ocean hideouts by filling their tiny tube feet, found underneath each arm, with seawater. Some scientists think their ancestors were feathery-armed sea lilies stuck to the sea floor by stems. Fossils have been found of wavy five-armed feeders with stems that date back hundreds of millions of years and which could be the ancient relatives of starfish. Back then, all life on Earth lived in the ocean and they would have shared their watery homes with fearsome sea monsters, such as sea scorpions the size of humans.

(2) Jellyfish

Jellyfish light up Earth's oceans with their trailing tentacles, beautiful bells and special stingers. With no bones, brain, lungs or heart, 95% of a jellyfish's body is made of water. By studying these remarkable creatures, scientists have made new discoveries about the past. One secret uncovered is around sleep. Most animals sleep because their brains need rest to recharge – but jellyfish sleep even though they do not have brains. This tells us that ancient animals may have slept even before they had brains.

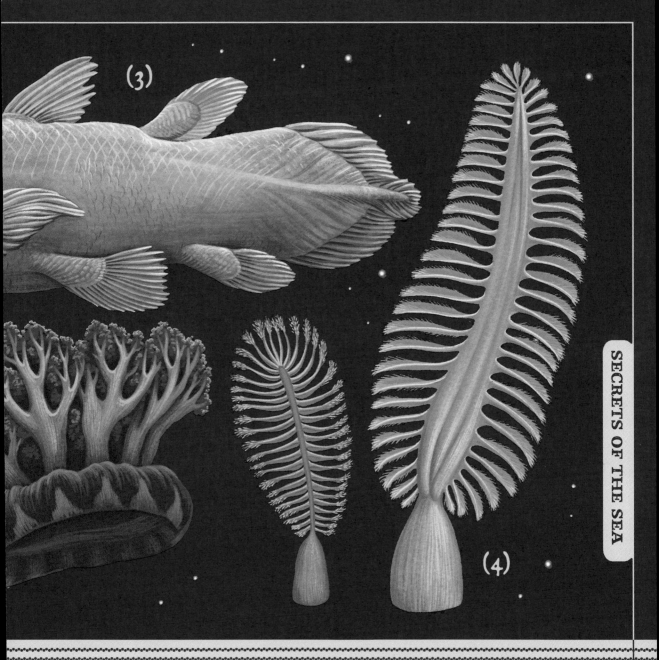

(3)

(4)

(3) Coelacanth

We once thought that these huge, deep-sea loving creatures had gone extinct around 65 million years ago, until a surprised captain and his crew caught one in a fishing net in 1938. Scientists think the coelacanth has not changed that much over millions of years, and its amazing scales, woven like armour, are usually found only on the fossils of fish that are extinct. This earned the coelacanth the nickname 'living fossil'. What is even more remarkable is that coelacanths are related to ancient tetrapods — and it is from these creatures that all land animals evolved.

(4) Sea pen

Spectacular multi-coloured sea pens may look similar to feathers, but are actually made of polyps (see page 7) that glow in the dark when touched. The polyps use their tentacles to catch food while the sea pen's bulbous body anchors itself in the sand. Scientists once thought that sea pens were related to Charnia (frond-like lifeforms), which lived about 550 million years ago, because they look so much like them. However, it turns out this is a total and extremely rare coincidence!

5

(1)

(3)

(1) Coral

Over 100 countries around the world have coral reefs covered in thousands of different types of brightly coloured coral, housing creatures called polyps. Polyps are tube-shaped with mouths and tentacles, and they are packed with evidence of Earth's history.

Coral has skeletons with rings. Because corals can live for many thousands of years, scientists can take samples of the coral to study the depth and colour of each ring and this can tell them what the weather was like thousands of years ago, too. Darker rings mean warmer temperatures.

(2) Seabed

Did you know that the different coloured layers of the seabed paint a picture of the past? Scientists study the layers and the details within reveal secrets. For instance, if a layer doesn't contain shells or micro-creature fossils (tiny remains of animals, plants and bacteria), then this tells us there might have been a massive extinction during that time.

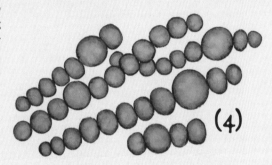

(4)

(3) Sea *sponge*

Sea sponges hide an amazing secret because they collect other animals' DNA. DNA is like the recipe for all the things that make a living creature work. Understanding it tells us the difference between creatures today and creatures that lived a long time ago, and how they are related. Sea sponges collect DNA while filtering seawater, which contains tissues and cells shed by other nearby creatures as they float through the water. So, sea sponges also tell us which animals live, or travel through, the waters around them. This helps scientists build a fuller picture of ocean ecosystems.

(4) Blue-green algae

Cyanobacteria, often called 'blue-green algae', are organisms that live in some seas (and ponds and lakes) and they hold the story of one of the most important things on Earth — oxygen, the gas we breathe to keep us alive. There used to be no oxygen on Earth until cyanobacteria produced it. Cyanobacteria don't just live in seas and oceans — they live in many habitats, including desert rocks, and can also be found in some species of tree lichen. Blue-green algae is *very* poisonous, so *never* touch it. Without oxygen, YOU would not exist!

(2)

Sharks

Hundreds of species of shark glide through the world's oceans. Most sharks have torpedo-shaped bodies adorned with V-shaped scales and clever fins that help them steer. A shark's skeleton is mostly made from tough, rubbery cartilage (a connective tissue also found in human bodies). It is all these things that give scientists clues about the incredible history of a shark...

Scientists think that around 450 million years ago, the ancestors of sharks were living as toothless swimmers that may have eventually evolved into a kind of creature called an acanthodian. Acanthodians were shark-like creatures that *did* have teeth, but they also had diamond-shaped scales that are very different from the shape of shark scales today. After that came what scientists call the 'golden age of sharks' 380 million years ago. A mass extinction caused most of Earth's creatures to die out, but the ancestors of sharks evolved to become the rulers of the seas. All kinds of weird and wonderful sharks evolved, including a shark called a Helicoprion that had a spiral-shaped saw for a jaw.

Over millions of years, scientists say sharks and their ancestors survived five mega extinctions, going from big to small... then to HUGE... until they finally evolved into the many shark-sized swimmers there are today. Now over 500 awe-inspiring species of shark swim along in our mysterious oceans...

Great white shark

Dwarf lantern shark

Mako shark

Dwarf lantern sharks have evolved to have light-up bellies, which may help them to attract prey, communicate with other lantern sharks and hide from predators. They are also smaller than a human hand! Why they evolved to be so small is a secret yet to be uncovered.

Goblin shark

Leopard shark

Whale shark

Greenland shark

At up to 500 years old, the Greenland shark of today is the oldest living creature in our oceans. Scientists can find out how old a Greenland shark is by measuring something called radioactive carbon in its eyes.

Basking shark

Saw shark

SECRETS OF THE ICE

Welcome to nature's frozen worlds, where penguins protect their eggs, polar bears prowl and seal pups swim and dive. It is no secret that Earth's iciest places are incredible, but ice also hides some of history's coldest, hottest and most remarkable secret stories. From mass extinctions to exploding volcanoes, from fossilised dinosaurs to ancient atmospheres, ice can tell us so much about our planet's past.

Ice cores can tell us Earth's secret history up to 800,000 years ago...

A thicker, darker layer of ice shows us that the world was colder at that time.

Volcanic dust trapped in an ice core told scientists that a huge volcano erupted in Greenland 50,000 years ago.

Trapped air bubbles tell us what gases were in the atmosphere, for example how much oxygen there was at that time.

The icy stories of Earth's past can help us think about its changing climate and its future. The secrets preserved in ice cores show we have the highest levels of carbon dioxide in 400,000 years.

A 4.6-billion-year-old meteorite fossil containing ice tells scientists that ice may have arrived here on asteroids.

Ice cores

Ice acts like a frozen time capsule that can help us piece together Earth's story. Dinosaurs, mammoths, plants and microbes have all been found fossilised in ice, but amazingly it can also tell us about the weather, the atmosphere and major events from thousands of years ago. Scientists can carefully remove giant cylinders, called ice cores, from glaciers. They then study the layers to find out when the whole world was covered in ice, which plants grew in ancient times, when vast volcanoes erupted and how much oxygen used to be on Earth.

A Cryolophosaurus dinosaur fossil was found in an icy Antarctic glacier by palaeontologists. It lived there millions of years ago when all the ice was a forest that wasn't cold at all!

(1)

(2)

(3)

(4)

(1) Colossal squid

Super-camouflaging squid hide deep in our oceans, and at as much as 14 metres long, the colossal squid is the most gigantic of them all! Squid are fast swimmers and have eight arm tentacles and two feeding tentacles that quickly shoot out to catch their prey, but in the past squid were much slower. Fossils show their ancestors carried shells on their backs, which made it more difficult to move with ease. Over time, these shells got smaller until they lost them. A heavy shell would have slowed these squid ancestors down, and they needed to be fast to catch prey before other, also evolving, ocean life caught it first — and to escape newly evolved predators!

(2) Polar bear

Shhh! Polar bears don't actually have white fur. Their skin is black and their hair is hollow. When the Sun shines, all the colours in light bounce off each hair, making it appear white. But a polar bear didn't always need this clever trick. A long time ago, when some brown-haired bears moved to icier places, their fur changed colour to match the new environment. Their ears and tails grew smaller too, so they'd lose less heat, which helps them stay warm — and *that* is why polar bears look the way they do today.

(3) Spotted seal

Spotted, harp, hooded, ringed, bearded and ribbon are all seals that live in an icy environment. These seals slide through icy water using their fantastic flippers, but did you know that seals once used to walk on four legs? Fossils of ancient seal ancestors that look like otters show seals used to have four legs and a long tail. Before seals became the blubbery beauties we know today, scientists also think they had webbed feet, flattened fur and teeth a bit like dogs.

(4) Emperor penguin

All kinds of penguin flip, flap, waddle and dive in icy waters. At over a metre tall, the biggest species is the emperor penguin, which boasts beautiful black and white feathers with yellow and orange on its head, neck and breast. Penguins probably use their black and white feathers to camouflage themselves from predators in dark waters that are covered in white ice. But scientists who have studied the fossils of an ancient adult penguin living 36 million years ago found its feathers to be mostly reddish-brown and grey — we don't yet know why these ancient penguins were a different colour. Fossils of extinct penguins have also been found with very long beaks, which they may have used to spear fish.

Blue whale

Beluga whale

Narwhal

Humpback whale

Whales are divided into
two main types — toothed whales,
such as sperm whales and beluga
whales, and baleen (or toothless)
whales, such as humpback whales
and blue whales. The male
narwhal's long tusk is
actually a tooth!

Scientists found some
26-million-year-old fossils of a
baleen whale ancestor: it lived in the
sea and had a flat nose similar to a
modern baleen whale (such as a blue
or humpback). However, the fossil also
showed it probably had tiny legs —
left over from when its ancestors
walked on land.

Whales

Whales are the biggest animals in the sea, and they keep a *big* secret about their past too... at one point, their ancestors lived on land! Their secret history is so well hidden that no one knows exactly how they moved from land to sea, only that they did. Slowly at first, probably living between land and freshwater, until eventually they ventured out into the big blue ocean.

Their bodies changed to be better suited to the sea and they evolved to become bigger and bigger until they grew *so* big that some became the largest animals, not just in the ocean, but also on Earth. Scientists discovered this secret story because of an ear...

After years of wondering where whales came from, they found fossils of an ancient hooved, dog-like beast they called a Pakicetid. After lots of investigation, it turned out the fossils of these ancient beasts had the same kind of ear as a whale!

And so, the tale of the whale that used to walk on land solved one of the biggest evolution mysteries of all time. Now there are many species of whale living in oceans and seas around the world, but *these* wonderful whales either live in, or migrate to, icy waters.

sperm whale

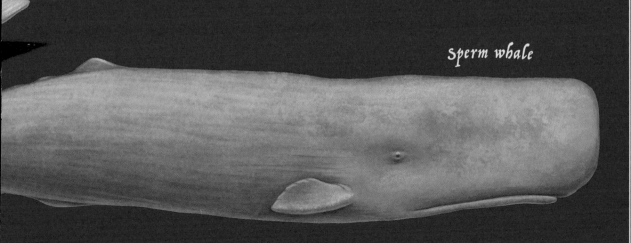

SECRETS OF THE FOREST

The world's forests are phenomenal. Ants of every colour guard a tale as old as time, mushrooms pass messages to each other underground and trees are homes to millions of secret ecosystems. Trees create the oxygen we need to breathe and can store carbon underground, then use it to build the things *they* need to create new trees, such as roots, trunks and stems. They communicate with each other in hidden ways, too. Mother trees feed their own seedlings with important carbon underground rather than passing it to a stranger, while wise old trees secretly pass messages to each other through their roots — paths along which chemicals can travel to tell other trees if danger or disease is nearby.

Fantastic forests also whisper stories of the past. Millions of years ago, the ancestors of ancient trees saw dinosaurs dashing along the forest floor and stopping to snap up their leaves...

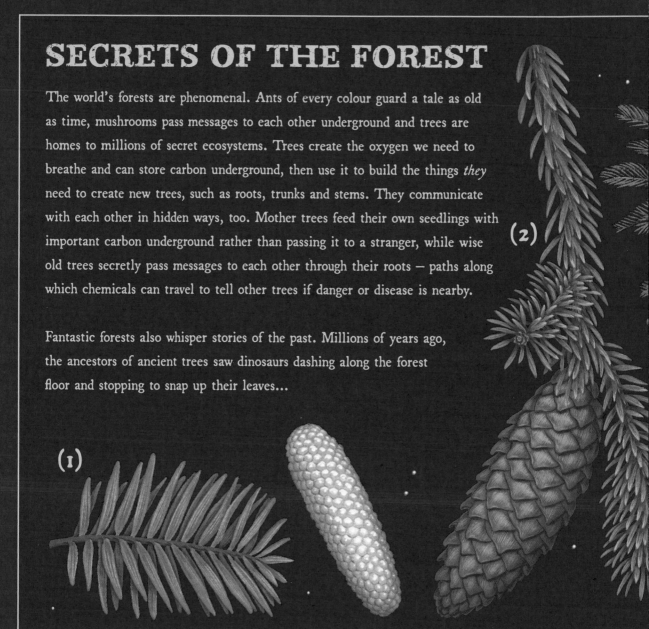

(1)

(2)

(1) Pine tree

Pines are one of the oldest species of tree on the planet. Today, squirrels and birds forage pinecones for food, but millions of years ago, the ancestors of pines were eaten by ancient beasts — long-necked sauropods feasted on high branches while other dinosaurs nibbled the needles that fell to the ground. We can tell how old a tree fossil is by using carbon dating. Trees absorb carbon from the air when they are alive. Scientists measure how much carbon is left in the fossil — the less carbon, the older the fossil.

(2) Conifer tree

Conifers have been on Earth for around 300 million years. During the age of the dinosaurs, they were a source of food for the spiky stegosaurs. Scientists know that these trees existed at the same time as dinosaurs by studying fossilised dinosaur poo. Some of these rare dinosaur poo fossils have been found with the rotten wood from conifers inside, which means that the dinosaurs ate the wood. These fossils tell us about *other* trees, too. Scientists think that because dinosaurs ate so many plants, the plants evolved to protect themselves — pinecones evolved to provide a well-protected armour around their seeds!

SECRETS OF THE FOREST

(3) Cycad tree

Stegosaurs and sauropods also fed on cycad trees. But cycads tell us about another dinosaur as well — Isaberrysaura — which had poo that was full of cycad seeds! Isaberrysaura looked like a stegosaur, but was actually a different type of dinosaur. It would have had to be careful not to get sick from the toxic centre of a cycad tree's seeds as they are highly poisonous, which tells scientists that its b[...] somehow fou[...]

(4) Tree fern

With their arching fronds and trunk-like stems, beautiful tree ferns hide an amazing history. Plants and trees take in carbon dioxide and produce and release oxygen, a[...] scientists think the ancestors of ferns were one of the [...] big land plants to do this — in fact, they helped to [...] the oxygen dinosaurs and other ancient beasts [...] evolve. It's also thought [...]
di[...]ch
[...]a time
[...]tter than today.

17

(1) Crocodile

Crocodiles are often referred to as 'living fossils' for a reason – they're one of the few animals on Earth not to have changed much in 80 million years. Their ancestors date all the way back to when dinosaurs roamed the Earth. These fierce predators have adapted to survive all kinds of environments and threats. Modern crocodiles, such as the Nile crocodile and saltwater crocodile, have among the most powerful bites on the planet, which provides one of the secrets to these reptiles' survival and success. If your bite is *that* powerful, it is easy to catch food without having to evolve too much over time.

(2) Woodland salamander

Woodland salamanders are astonishing tree climbers that grow to around 15 centimetres long. These tiny animals hold a *big* secret... they are descendants of the car-sized mighty Metoposaurus that hung out at the waterside, gobbling up the very first dinosaurs, before shrinking over time to become the small creatures that lounge around in trees today.

(3) Red and white giant flying squirrel

Flying squirrels glide from tree to tree using their unusual parachute-style features. And this species of flying squirrel was only very recently discovered! Scientists don't think flying squirrels have changed much over millions and millions of years, carefully guarding the yet-to-be-uncovered secrets of their ancestors. Seeing as these ancestors lived at a time when elephants had four tusks (twice as many as modern elephants), this makes them pretty unique!

(4) Wood turtle

These turtles are known for their beautiful shells, which look like intricately engraved wood. The turtles rely on their shells for shelter and protection. But many years ago, turtles didn't have shells and they looked a bit like lizards instead. Over time, turtles grew shells to help them dig in soil and sand. Now they dig with their legs and use their shells to hide in.

(1)

(2)

(3)

(4)

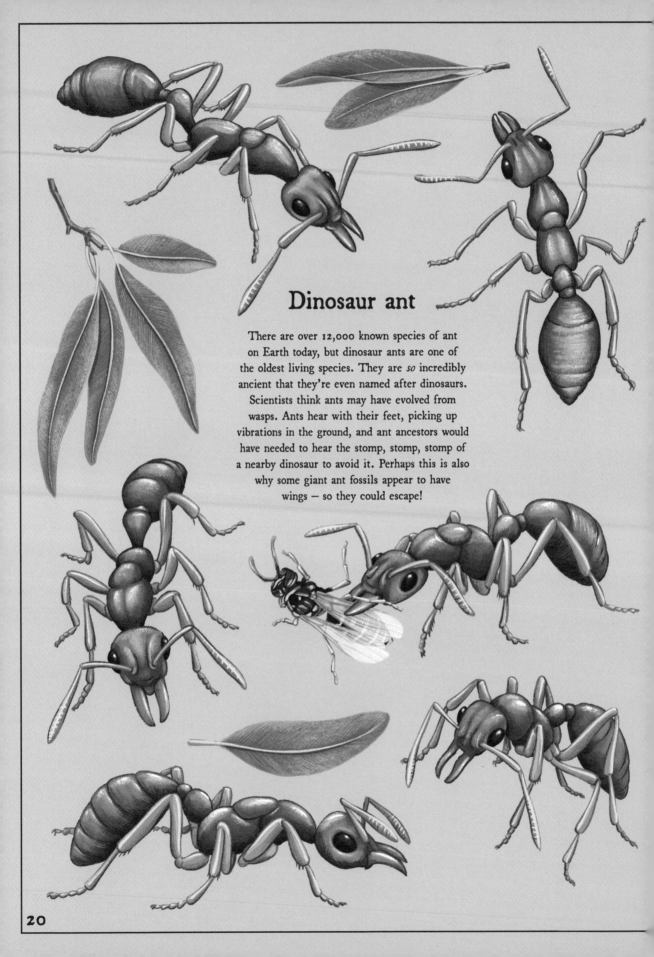

Dinosaur ant

There are over 12,000 known species of ant on Earth today, but dinosaur ants are one of the oldest living species. They are *so* incredibly ancient that they're even named after dinosaurs. Scientists think ants may have evolved from wasps. Ants hear with their feet, picking up vibrations in the ground, and ant ancestors would have needed to hear the stomp, stomp, stomp of a nearby dinosaur to avoid it. Perhaps this is also why some giant ant fossils appear to have wings — so they could escape!

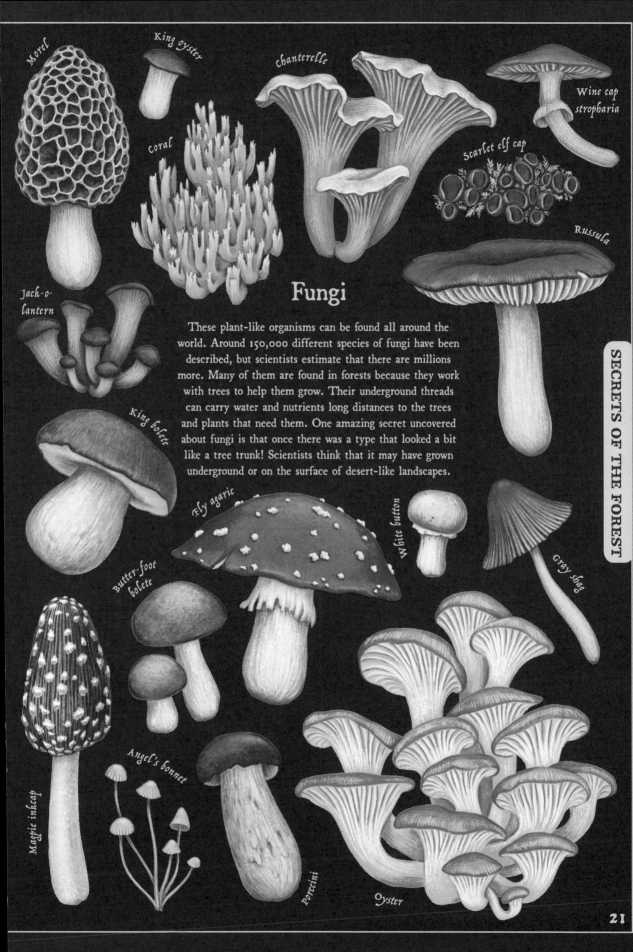

Morel

King oyster

Chanterelle

Wine cap
stropharia

Coral

Scarlet elf cap

Russula

Jack-o-
lantern

Fungi

These plant-like organisms can be found all around the world. Around 150,000 different species of fungi have been described, but scientists estimate that there are millions more. Many of them are found in forests because they work with trees to help them grow. Their underground threads can carry water and nutrients long distances to the trees and plants that need them. One amazing secret uncovered about fungi is that once there was a type that looked a bit like a tree trunk! Scientists think that it may have grown underground or on the surface of desert-like landscapes.

King bolete

Fly agaric

White button

Gray shag

Butter-foot
bolete

Magpie inkcap

Angel's bonnet

Porcini

Oyster

SECRETS OF THE JUNGLE

Tropical forests and jungles are magnificent worlds where elephants roam, monkeys laugh and leopards lounge. But vast areas of jungle are cut down every year, destroying the homes of the animals that live there. It is a devastating loss of a place that can tell us so much about the past. A long time ago, in a climate suited to dinosaurs and ancient beasts, tropical forests stretched further than you might think possible, even as far as the icy South Pole. Today, half of the world's species can be found in rainforests and they are full of secret stories – including those of our close relatives, apes.

(1) Lemur

Lemurs leap from tree to tree in tropical rainforests. They have a very special secret link... with *you*! Scientists think that the very first primates on Earth belonged to the lemur family. Because humans evolved from a type of primate, some scientists think that lemurs are one of our distant cousins. Today, lemurs live only in tropical forests on the African island of Madagascar. Scientists think they floated there from mainland Africa millions of years ago, using rafts made of vegetation.

(2) Orangutan

These beautiful orange apes like to stay in trees as much as possible, unlike their early ancestor, Sivapithecus. Scientists think that Sivapithecus spent much more time on the ground. Orangutans keep their babies close to them and like humans, they have a hairline – maybe that's because these furry beasts also share *our* family tree! In fact, scientists think humans and orangutans share 97% of the same DNA.

(4)

(3)

(3) Peacock spider

The beautiful peacock spider lives in the jungle and is one of around 50,000 different species of spider living on our planet. While piecing together the secret history of the spider, scientists discovered the fossils of an ancient spider relative with a whip-like tail! The spider probably used the tail to sense its surroundings. As we are discovering new animals all the time, perhaps we will find a *living* spider with a tail one day!

(4) Elephant

Did you know that an elephant's footprint can help us discover secrets of the past? The footprints of the fossils of ancient animals can tell us where that animal was going and whether it was alone or with others. Elephants live in herds, so we usually see lots of elephant footprints together. When scientists find lots of dinosaur footprints together, such as those of hadrosaurs, they know that they also lived in herds. Once they know a dinosaur lived in a herd, scientists look at modern herd animals to give them clues about how that dinosaur might have behaved. Elephants stay together to help keep themselves safe — maybe that's what dinosaurs did, too.

Strawberry poison-dart frog

Green and black
poison-dart frog

Frogs

Once upon a time, the ancient relatives of these curious little creatures
were as big as alligators and as lethal as crocodiles — scientists have even found
ancient frog-type fossils as big as cars! That's because frogs share the same
swampy, dinosaur-munching ancestor as salamanders — Metoposaurus (see page 18).
Scientists have also found frog fossils from later in dinosaur times that are only as
big as beach balls, while teeny-tiny frog-like creatures that also lived
alongside dinosaurs have been found trapped in tree sap.

So... we are still piecing together the fantastic frog's ancient history,
but one thing most scientists seem to agree on is what happened to frogs
after dinosaurs. The asteroid that wiped out the dinosaurs gave frogs a chance
to flourish. Almost all the ancestors of the different species of frog we see today
appear to have evolved at the same time after dinosaurs disappeared.
Scientists call this time 'the rise of the frogs'.

Modern frogs of many colours also hide a secret —
their different-shaped skulls have evolved in amazing ways to defend
themselves or to catch prey. Horned tree frogs have bony spikes hidden in
their skulls, shovel-headed tree frogs use their heads as shields and
casque-headed frogs store venom in their skulls
to spike predators!

Shovel-headed tree frog

Horned tree frog

Casque-headed tree frog

Red-eyed tree frog

White-lipped tree frog

Pumpkin frog

Glass frog

Blue poison-dart frog

Tomato frog

Tiger

Ocelot

Bengal and Sumatran
tigers are jungle-
dwelling big cats.
They are both in
danger of extinction.

Black panther

Jaguars are found in the Amazon rainforest and nearby wetlands.

Jaguar

Wild cats

Beautiful wild cats use their markings, such as stripes and spots, to camouflage themselves so they can stalk and sneak up on their prey without being noticed. Incredibly, scientists studying the secrets of these cats have found that these magnificent creatures didn't always have spots and stripes. Instead, they evolved slowly over time to suit their different habitats, including the jungle homes of the species shown here. Today, leopards, jaguars and ocelots across continents use their spots to hide in branches bathed in dappled sunlight. Tigers' stripes are perfect for sheltering them in shaded forests and long grass, while the dark coats of nocturnal black panthers help them hide as they hunt in the night.

Camouflaging creatures can even tell us secrets about *other* beasts of the ancient past, such as dinosaurs. Scientists have found some colour pigments preserved in dinosaur fossils but can't be sure exactly what dinosaurs looked like, since no one has ever seen one alive! So, scientists use animals that exist today as proxies (something used to represent something else). Once they find dinosaur fossils, they use special techniques to build up a picture of the dinosaur's habitat millions of years ago, then they wonder if the dinosaur would have needed to be camouflaged in that habitat. They use real-life animals from similar habitats today as examples of what dinosaurs *might* have looked like or how they may have behaved.

As well as living in the jungles of West and Central Africa, leopards live in grasslands, deserts and savannahs in India and Asia.

Leopard

SECRETS OF THE MOUNTAINS

Magnificent mountains peer over our incredible Earth like ladders to the clouds. But mountains are not only above ground. While some mountains are covered in snowy peaks, volcanoes (which are types of mountains) bubble away with hot lava from deep inside the Earth, and there are also mountains to be found under the sea. Mountains are home to many different creatures, from big brown bears to tough tardigrades, and they include many different habitats, such as frozen peaks, mountainous deserts and volcanic soil. They are also made from the very crust of our ancient planet...

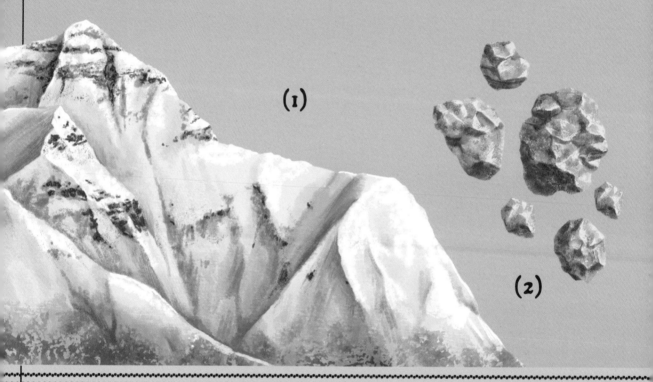

(1)

(2)

(1) Mount Everest

With its peak at 8,849 metres above sea level, Mount Everest is the tallest mountain in the world. But this high mountain top also has an enormous secret story to tell — it used to be an ocean floor! Scientists uncovered this mystery when they took samples from the top of Everest to find that they contained marine limestone and fossils of ancient ocean life, which means rocks on Mount Everest were once covered in water.

(2) Limestone

Marine limestone is a type of rock that is formed of layers of tiny shells, skeletons, plant matter and mud. Over time, the layers are compressed by seawater and harden into rock. The limestone samples found on the summit (the highest point) of Everest contain fragments of the fossils of ancient sea creatures and plants that existed hundreds of millions of years ago, possibly in shallow waters.

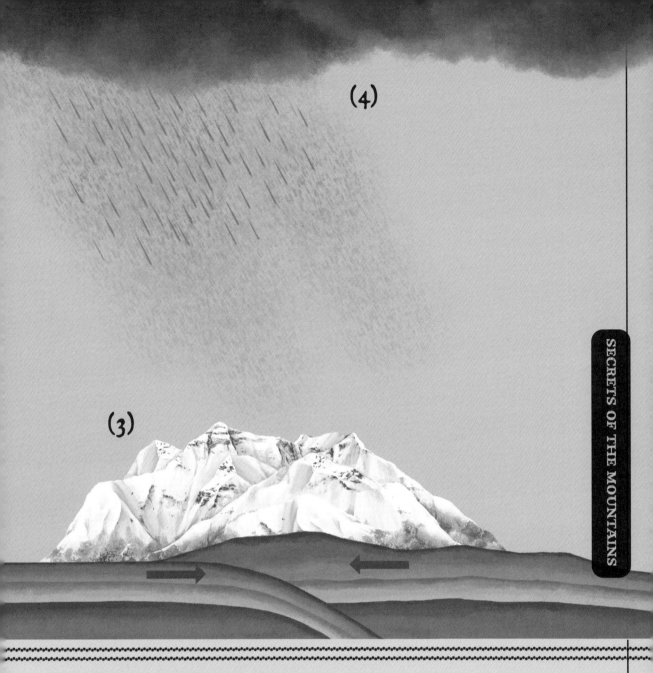

(4)

(3)

(3) How mountains form

Scientists used the evidence of mountain-top marine limestone to piece together the puzzle of how mountains might have formed. The Earth's crust (outer layer) is broken up into things called plates. These plates sometimes smash against each other and when this happens mountains form above ground. Mount Everest was probably made when a plate that had broken away from its land mass collided with Asia. The collision pushed up the land to create the Himalayan Mountain Range, which is home to Mount Everest. These plates are still colliding today, which means Mount Everest is actually growing taller each year!

(4) Weather

Mountains have another secret story — they can change the weather. Air rising over the mountains cools down, creating clouds and rain on one side of the mountain. Dry air flows down the other side of the mountain, creating an extremely dry 'rain shadow'. The mountain shadows one side from rain, sometimes even creating a desert!

(1) North American porcupine

These tree-needle nibblers live in forested areas that are often found in mountain ranges. The North American porcupine is the largest of all porcupines and has around 30,000 sharp quills. It spends most of its time in trees eating bark, stems, fruit and leaves. Porcupines evolved from ancient rodents that did not have quills. Their secret weapons were stiff hairs that changed over time to become sharp quills used to protect them.

(2) Alpine grasshoper

With ears on their bellies that listen out for the tunes of other grasshoppers, these insects hop around all kinds of habitats, including mountains, on every continent except Antarctica. But scientists think that millions of years ago grasshoppers had just one home — South America, after they evolved there from their ancient ancestors. Then they somehow 'hopped' over to Africa, which was then covered in tropical rainforests, even though there was already a sea between the two continents! (Africa and South America used to be part of one supercontinent called Gondwana.)

(3) Tardigrade

Is anything tougher than a tardigrade? These tiny eight-legged animals, also called 'water bears' or 'moss piglets', are amazing adaptors that can survive almost all environments on the planet, including the highest mountains and volcanic vents in the oceans. They can survive for up to 30 years without food or water and their bodies produce a type of antifreeze to protect them from harsh environments. Scientists believe their secret story spans over 500 million years of life on Earth, but because their bodies decay so quickly it is very rare to find a fossil. The oldest one to date is 16 million years old and it's just one of three ever found.

(4) Brown bear

Big brown bears are one of the largest animals on Earth, and they're said to have one of the strongest bite forces in the entire animal kingdom! When they are young, brown bears can climb trees — a bit like their small, dog-cat-like ancestors from the Miacidae family, which had monkey-type tails and scurried up trees. Over time, bears lost their long tails — they no longer needed them. Tails help an animal balance and turn with ease, so they were useful to the smaller ancestors of bears, which had to run and climb to escape bigger predators.

(1)

(2)

(3)

(4)

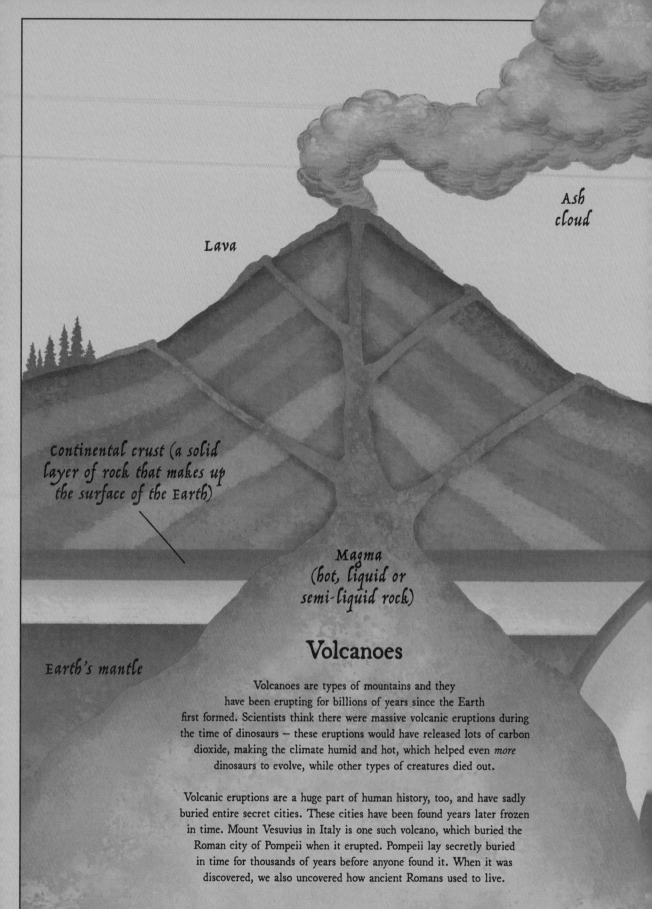

Ash
cloud

Lava

Continental crust (a solid
layer of rock that makes up
the surface of the Earth)

Magma
(hot, liquid or
semi-liquid rock)

Earth's mantle

Volcanoes

Volcanoes are types of mountains and they
have been erupting for billions of years since the Earth
first formed. Scientists think there were massive volcanic eruptions during
the time of dinosaurs — these eruptions would have released lots of carbon
dioxide, making the climate humid and hot, which helped even *more*
dinosaurs to evolve, while other types of creatures died out.

Volcanic eruptions are a huge part of human history, too, and have sadly
buried entire secret cities. These cities have been found years later frozen
in time. Mount Vesuvius in Italy is one such volcano, which buried the
Roman city of Pompeii when it erupted. Pompeii lay secretly buried
in time for thousands of years before anyone found it. When it was
discovered, we also uncovered how ancient Romans used to live.

Underwater volcanoes

You might not think that something as huge and powerful as a volcano could hide, but believe it or not some volcanoes secretly lurk underwater. They have *huge* secrets too — when they erupt, they have been known to make entire islands! Mauna a Wakea is one of 15 volcanoes that erupted to make the eight islands of Hawai'i as far back as 70 million years ago, when magma started to burst from the sea surface and cooled to form the islands. Mauna a Wakea is actually taller than Mount Everest. It is so tall that it lives both above ground *and* underwater...

Ocean

Oceanic crust (the part of the Earth's crust that makes up the ocean floor)

Earth's mantle (a layer of very hot, almost solid rock)

Hot magma forces the oceanic crust open

SECRETS OF THE SKY

A wonderful world is waiting in the skies that surround us. Curious clouds create the water we need to survive, butterflies and bees flit and skitter from branch to stem, and birds soar with the secret story that they all evolved from dinosaurs.

Why do we see the sky as beautiful blue? That's another secret that's been revealed. It's because when sunlight (which is all the colours of the rainbow) hits the gases and particles in Earth's atmosphere, it scatters the blue light more than the other colours. But billions of years ago, the atmosphere we know today did not exist and neither did the sky...

(2)

(1)

(1) Sunlight

Earth's closest star, the Sun, holds one of the most spectacular secret stories of all — that of why our planet exists. It was created by the Sun! Before our solar system was created, the gravity from the Sun pulled clumps of matter together to form all of its planets, including Earth. Most living things on Earth need sunlight to survive. It provides warmth, energy and light that we cannot get anywhere else.

(2) Cloud

Clouds are created when the Sun heats up water. Billions of years ago when the Earth was formed, there was no liquid water on the planet — it was too hot! So, clouds (as we know them today) did not exist. We know this because it takes water to *make* a cloud, even though clouds themselves create water (water vapour rises from oceans and lakes and cools down to form a cloud of water droplets, which join together to form heavy raindrops that eventually burst out). Thanks to this, called the 'water cycle', today we can see all kinds of different types of cloud, from puffy-looking cumulus clouds to hot hurricane clouds and flat-bottomed fog.

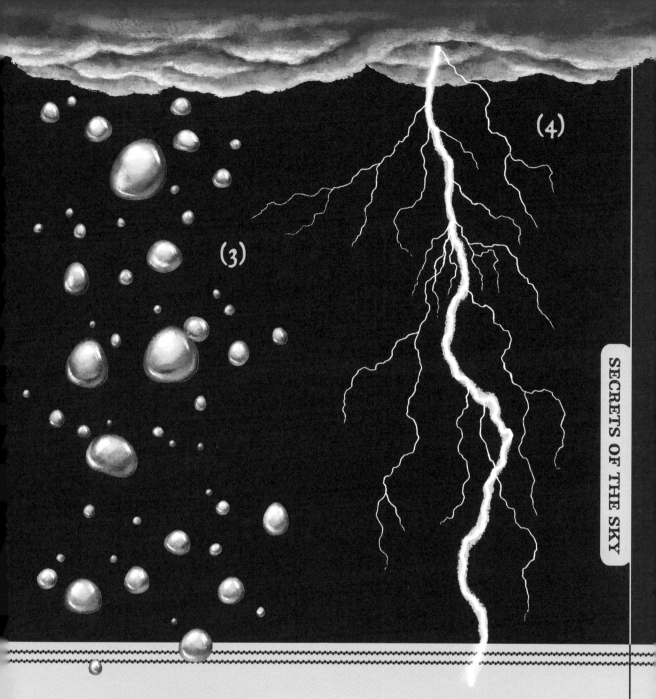

(3) Raindrop

Even a drop of rain can tell nature's stories. Raindrops are made in a cloud and when they start to fall, they are not tear-shaped — this happens as they increase speed on the way to the ground. But even more amazing is their secret history. Some scientists believe it may have once rained for two million years thanks to a massive volcanic eruption and that this immense amount of rain kickstarted the evolution of dinosaurs.

(4) Lightning

Lightning storms that fire up our sky look extraordinary. But it's even more incredible to spot fossilised lightning. When lightning strikes sand it can make something called a fulgurite, which turns the lightning into a fossil. These fossils tell us how far back in our planet's history lightning storms took place and what the weather was like at that time. You need hot weather for a lightning storm, so once scientists have confirmed how old the fossil is, they have an idea of how hot it was at that time, too.

35

Birds

Look up at the sky and it won't be long before you spot a bird —
a swooping, soaring, diving, dodging, bewitching bird, holding on to
one of the biggest secrets of animal history ever.

For the beautiful birds that fill our skies today are actually
descended from dinosaurs. This secret began to unravel when scientists
found the fossils of an ancient feathery beast called Archaeopteryx, a
chicken-sized creature with dinosaur teeth and a dinosaur tail, *but* with
brilliant bird-like wings. Scientists began looking more closely at dinosaurs,
especially a group called the therapods. They realised that most of these therapods
— including the super-swift carnivore Velociraptor — had feathers, which we
know because quill (part of a feather) markings have been found in their
fossilised bones. Velociraptors had claws like birds of prey, too!

Scientists believe that once dinosaurs and other ancient beasts began to
have feathers, they started shrinking fast and then — over millions of years —
eventually turned into the thousands of bird species flying in our skies today.
And so it came to be that birds, the amazing descendants of some of the most
fearful beasts on Earth, no longer have monstrous teeth, or whip-like tails
and aren't so fearful after all. (Unless of course you count the
secretary bird, which stamps on snakes...)

Toucan

Mallard

Raven

Secretary bird

Wren

Egret

Osprey

Gull

Jay

Robin

Hummingbird

Woodpecker

Owl

Pigeon

37

(1) Dragonfly

Over 5,000 different types of dragonfly dart around the planet, grabbing prey with their feet. They reach speeds of up to 50 kilometres per hour by flapping their wings, which can span 5–20 centimetres across. But millions of years ago, an ancestor of a dragonfly had a wingspan of around 65–75 centimetres! And a secret lies in those used-to-be-giant winged creatures. Dragonflies (and other insects) have tubes in their body to carry oxygen. The more oxygen in the air, the bigger the size of the insect. Millions of years ago, there used to be more oxygen in the air — which could be why these ancestors were so ginormous.

(2) Wasp

Scientists think the ancestors of wasps lived alongside the dinosaurs hundreds of millions of years ago. Fossils of wasps found entombed in amber show that tens of millions of years ago, they looked a lot like the wasps we know today, which bring insect prey back to their burrows before chopping it up to serve as a tasty tea for their babies. Wasps may not have changed much for tens of millions of years, *but* one of their biggest secrets is that they're the ancestors of bees!

(3) Bee

Bees once looked and acted like ancient wasps that hunted other insects to turn into their supper... that was before they evolved to become vegetarians! A long, long time ago, the world had no flowers for bees to visit, which is why their ancestors ate other insects. However, when flowers started to grow, bees began to evolve — their tongues grew longer and their appetites turned less meaty until eventually they were buzzing from flower to flower, pollinating the Earth's plants like they do today.

(4) Butterfly

As with many creatures, the secret story of how butterflies evolved is not completely revealed. Some scientists think that they might have evolved from moths, possibly to escape prowling night predators such as the ancestors of bats. Others believe that they may have evolved because brilliant bees had evolved from wasps to pollinate the flowers on which butterflies could feed.

(3)

Bumblebee

Honey bee

(4)

SECRETS OF THE NIGHT

Night-time is here and while we are sleeping the spectacle of space comes to life. The Moon shines, stars twinkle and glitter and maybe a comet can be seen launching its fiery tail through the night. How many secret stories of the past are hidden in the dark?

The stars you can see are just a handful of the trillions in space, born billions of years ago in atomic clouds. When our solar system was created, the stars in one of these clouds sucked a lot of stuff together into a flat disc, which we call The Milky Way galaxy, and within this galaxy is our Sun. The Sun's gravity pulled together eight planets that include Earth. Even though you can't see our Sun at night, without it, night-time would not exist and neither would we...

(2)

(1)

When stars are born, scientists think that something called dark matter helps to build them, but dark matter is *so* secret no one has ever actually seen it.

(1) Star

Stars made our planet, Earth, which is a stunning secret in itself, but their most spectacular secret story is that stars also made YOU. Stars are made from hydrogen and helium atoms, two important elements, and the explosion of stars made almost all the *other* elements in our universe — the elements that make up everything on Earth, including you.

(2) Meteor

Meteors are space rocks that sometimes hurtle through space like showers in the dark sky. Some move slowly and have beautiful trains — others are fireballs or are fast and bright. Whatever the speed, meteors carry secrets in the form of ancient rock that sometimes lands on Earth. It contains the very building blocks of life. When a meteor lands on Earth, it is called a meteorite and it is thanks to these billion-year-old rocks that we know things such as why the centre of our Earth came to have a metal core — melted iron and nickel sank to its middle to form the core.

(4)

(3)

(3) Comet

Comets are frozen balls of ancient dust and gas that you can sometimes see at night. They're *so* ancient that they're actually left over from when our solar system first formed billions of years ago. Comets become hotter as they get closer to the Sun until their dust and gas turns into a fiery tail millions of kilometres long. They sometimes land on Earth and because they have been preserved in space for so long, they bring with them secrets of space past just like meteorites. Their materials tell us which elements existed when our solar system was first created.

(4) Moon

If you gaze at the Moon in the night sky, you might be able to see different shades of grey. Once upon a time, violent volcanoes on the Moon's surface used to erupt with lava. The grey patches you can see are actually ancient lava from a long time ago. Darker areas on the Moon are the craters left over from collisions. All these things give scientists secret clues as to how our Moon was made in the first place. It is likely to have been made when Earth crashed into another planet a long time ago.

Racoon

Bush baby

Racoons
can swim
and like
to hunt
fish.

Opossum

We know that mammals evolved from reptiles,
but we do not know why pangolins are the only
mammal to have reptilian-like scales! Illegal
poaching and habitat loss mean these
secret-keepers are now endangered.

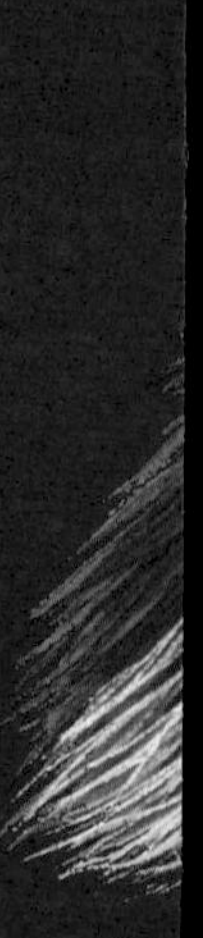

Bilby

Pangolin

Aardvark

Deer
mouse

Badger

Nocturnal mammals

Mammals are warm-blooded creatures with hair that produce milk for their young — for example, humans are mammals. But it turns out mammals' ancient ancestors are actually mammal-like reptiles! Scientists think mammals evolved from a group of reptiles called therapsids hundreds of millions of years ago, and that these therapsids became nocturnal (active at night) possibly to avoid their rivals, the dinosaurs. Therapsids eventually became extinct, but not before they gave rise to the ancestors of mammals.

Millions of years ago, the earliest mammals were probably most active at night too, to avoid the deadly dinosaurs that were active during the day. But when the massive asteroid hit Earth and giant waves tore across the land, space dust covered Earth and much of the planet was set on fire, dinosaurs could not survive.

Lots of mammals were wiped out too, but some mammals hid away in their underground burrows, surviving the dark and deadly years that followed. Or at least this is a scientist's best guess. For these mammals were also well adapted to the dark. After many, many years, mammals evolved to be the most successful *day*-loving creatures on Earth — humans.

But scientists also say that even now, millions of years later, most mammals still have eyes that are better suited to night. Some mammals still prefer to roam around pretty much only at night rather than during the day, just like these ones...

Skunks fire out their smelly spray up to 5 metres away.

Hedgehog

Spotted Skunk

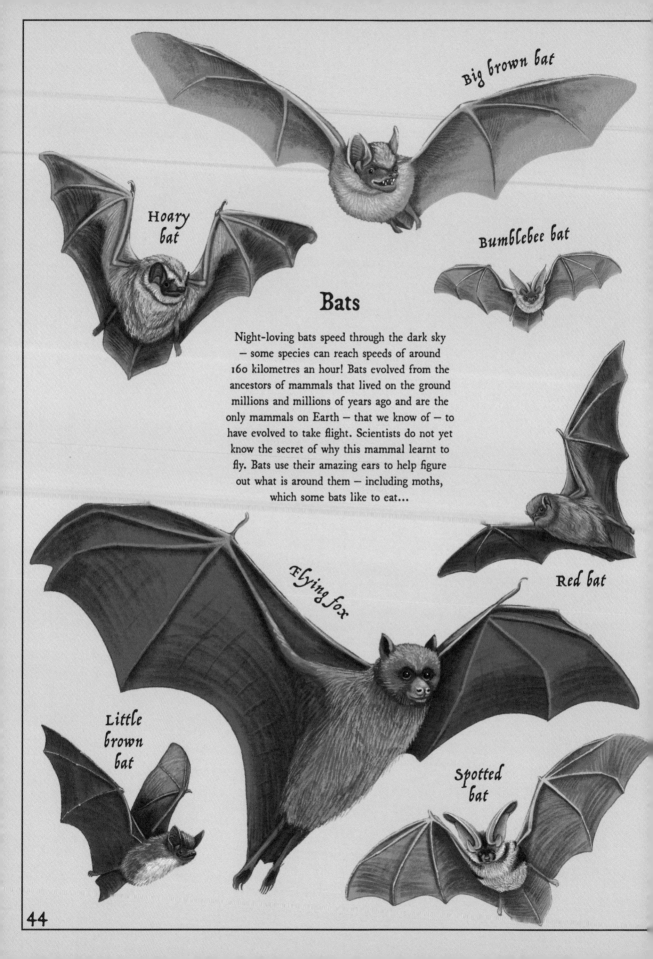

Big brown bat

Hoary bat

Bumblebee bat

Bats

Night-loving bats speed through the dark sky
— some species can reach speeds of around
160 kilometres an hour! Bats evolved from the
ancestors of mammals that lived on the ground
millions and millions of years ago and are the
only mammals on Earth — that we know of — to
have evolved to take flight. Scientists do not yet
know the secret of why this mammal learnt to
fly. Bats use their amazing ears to help figure
out what is around them — including moths,
which some bats like to eat...

Red bat

Flying fox

Little brown bat

Spotted bat

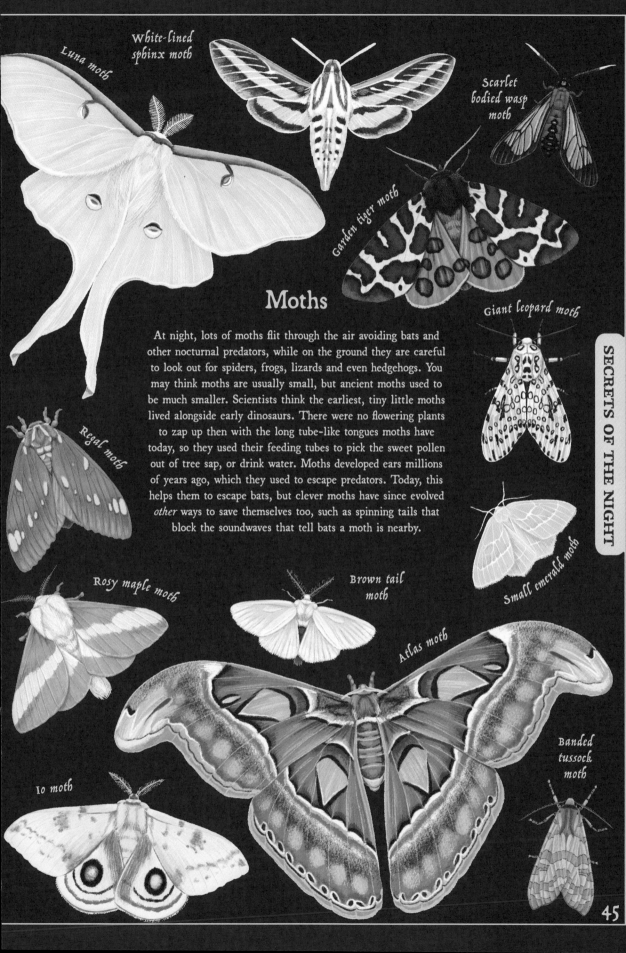

Luna moth

White-lined sphinx moth

Scarlet bodied wasp moth

Garden tiger moth

Giant leopard moth

Regal moth

Moths

At night, lots of moths flit through the air avoiding bats and other nocturnal predators, while on the ground they are careful to look out for spiders, frogs, lizards and even hedgehogs. You may think moths are usually small, but ancient moths used to be much smaller. Scientists think the earliest, tiny little moths lived alongside early dinosaurs. There were no flowering plants to zap up then with the long tube-like tongues moths have today, so they used their feeding tubes to pick the sweet pollen out of tree sap, or drink water. Moths developed ears millions of years ago, which they used to escape predators. Today, this helps them to escape bats, but clever moths have since evolved *other* ways to save themselves too, such as spinning tails that block the soundwaves that tell bats a moth is nearby.

Rosy maple moth

Brown tail moth

Small emerald moth

Atlas moth

Banded tussock moth

Io moth

SECRETS UNDERFOOT

Deep in the ground, inside the soil or hiding under leaves, lies a vibrant and busy world. Lots of creatures live underground and lots of animals live in the ground buried in burrows, leaves or mud, for many different reasons. Sometimes they are nocturnal and need a safe, warm place to hide away from predators, sometimes it is to hibernate over the long winter, sometimes it is to keep cool during the day. One thing is for sure, wherever we live in the world, there are many secret stories to be uncovered right under our feet...

(1)

(1) Royal python

Royal pythons are just one of many different types of snakes that like to live in burrows. There are thousands of different slithering species of snake in the world today and scientists have found some fossils of snakes that show they used to have back legs! Some snakes today such as pythons and boa constrictors still even have the tiniest remains of back leg bones near their tails.

(2) Australian spiral burrow scorpion

This type of scorpion lives in a spiral burrow feeding on burrowing spiders! There are around 2,000 different species of scorpion and their ancient history is amazing. Their ancestors lived in the ocean millions of years ago at a time when ALL our ancestors lived in the sea, but they were one of the *first* creatures to crawl out of the sea and start living on land. This led the way for other animals to do the same.

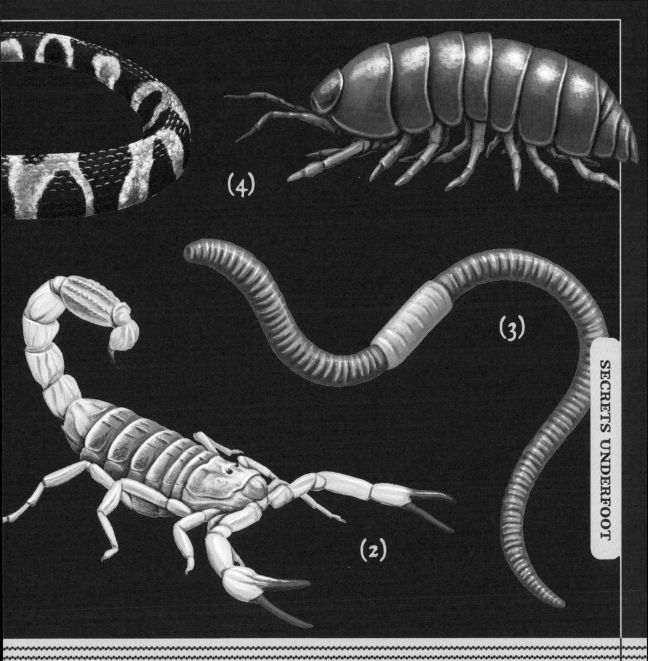

(4)

(3)

(2)

(3) Earthworm

Earthworms are secretly Earth's biggest heroes and creature creators. Worm burrows provide channels for oxygen in the soil, helping plant life stay healthy, which is vital for all of us. Knowing how key worms are to today's natural world, scientists think it's likely that worms could have helped Earth after the dinosaur-destroying asteroid hit Earth too, by bringing soil and seabeds back to life, which provided food for animals.

(4) Woodlouse

Woodlice have changed a lot from their much larger ancient relatives, trilobites — which lived on the seabed and had eyes in their cheeks! Woodlice have eyes on the sides of their heads to detect light, shade and large moving objects. They are sensitive to sunshine, which is why they like dark places. Unlike trilobites, they cannot swim — but they do breathe in air through gills, like many underwater creatures! Perhaps this is because they evolved from trilobites.

Brown rat

chipmunk

European hamster

Grey squirrel

Rodents

Although they look different, capybaras and mice come from the same family — rodents. And rodents are one of the most successful types of creature on Earth. Their ancestors were clever adaptors that survived the massive asteroid that killed off the dinosaurs and they now make up around 40% of Earth's mammal species!

The ancestors of rodents used to run around on one big supercontinent, Pangaea, before it separated into the continents we have today. These first rodent-like creatures were in a group called eutherians, and scientists think humans may share this same ancestor. This means that rodents including mice and rats share DNA with humans.

Harvest mouse

Capybara

Jerboa

Groundhog

The platypus digs its home along rivers and streams in Australia. With a bill like a duck, feet like an otter and a tail like a beaver, this egg-laying mammal is one of the most unique creatures in the history of evolution.

Platypus

Sir David's long-beaked echidna

Monotremes

Once upon a time, the ancestors of mammals lay eggs. Modern mammals give birth to young (rather than eggs from which their young hatch, like reptiles and birds). But there is one type of mammal left on Earth that never stopped laying eggs — monotremes. Platypus and echidna are all that is left of these egg-laying mammals. They have all the features of other mammals (they have hair and they feed their young with milk), but they still lay eggs.

Scientists call this 'mosaic evolution'. This is when over time there is a huge change in one creature in lots of ways, while other things remain the same. For example, humans learnt how to walk upright before their brains got bigger. We do not know why these monotremes carried on laying eggs. Recently scientists discovered a new secret about platypus, too — that their fur glows in the dark!

Eastern long-beaked echidna

Short-beaked echidna

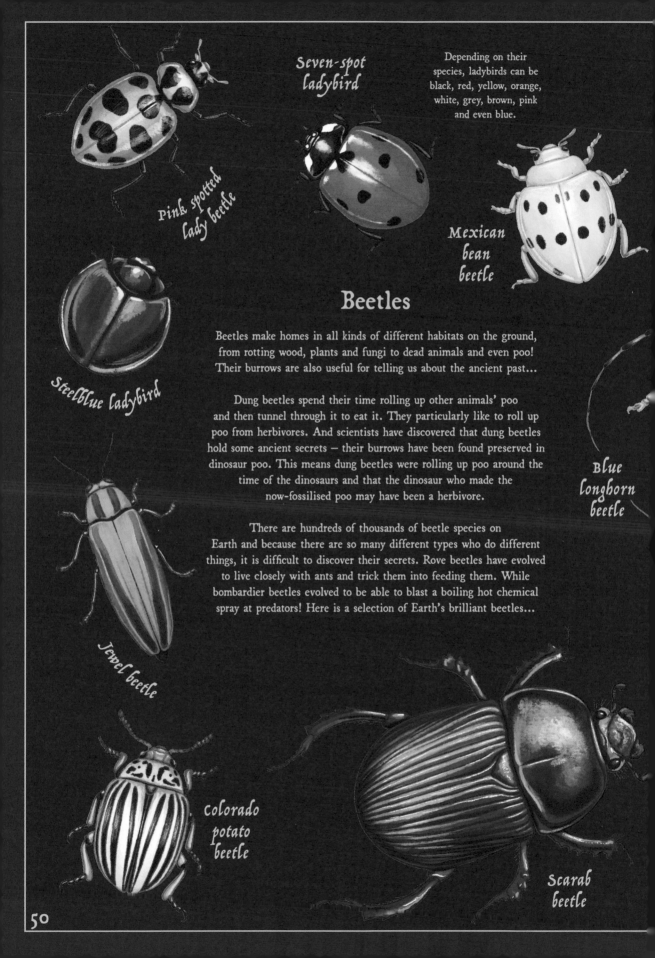

Seven-spot ladybird

Depending on their species, ladybirds can be black, red, yellow, orange, white, grey, brown, pink and even blue.

Pink spotted lady beetle

Mexican bean beetle

Steelblue ladybird

Beetles

Beetles make homes in all kinds of different habitats on the ground, from rotting wood, plants and fungi to dead animals and even poo! Their burrows are also useful for telling us about the ancient past...

Dung beetles spend their time rolling up other animals' poo and then tunnel through it to eat it. They particularly like to roll up poo from herbivores. And scientists have discovered that dung beetles hold some ancient secrets – their burrows have been found preserved in dinosaur poo. This means dung beetles were rolling up poo around the time of the dinosaurs and that the dinosaur who made the now-fossilised poo may have been a herbivore.

There are hundreds of thousands of beetle species on Earth and because there are so many different types who do different things, it is difficult to discover their secrets. Rove beetles have evolved to live closely with ants and trick them into feeding them. While bombardier beetles evolved to be able to blast a boiling hot chemical spray at predators! Here is a selection of Earth's brilliant beetles...

Blue longhorn beetle

Jewel beetle

Colorado potato beetle

Scarab beetle

The bombardier beetle has evolved to defend itself by firing out chemicals from its abdomen that can explode in the air!

Bombardier beetle

Stag beetle

Titan beetle

With a body length that can be well over 16 centimetres, the titan is one of the world's largest beetles. But much of its life remains a mystery — even though its larvae must be very large too, as far as we know no one has *ever* seen one.

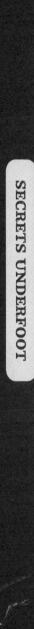

Weevil

Dogbane beetle

SEARCHING FOR SECRETS

Now you know that everything in nature has a secret story, you can do some discovering of your own. What wildlife can you observe close to home? What secrets does it reveal? Maybe you will uncover something no one else has yet...

Remember to respect the natural world as you interact with it, and make sure to keep yourself safe on your search for nature's secrets. Do not disturb animals or nests, wear gloves, never eat, pick or handle unknown plants, fungi, berries or other nature objects, and make sure to explore nature with an adult's help.

Seashells

Lots of different types of empty shells wash up on the beach. Which creatures used to live in them?

Tests

These curious, colourful specimens used to be shells of ocean animals such as sea urchins.

Mermaid's purses

Shark or skate eggs
and embryos develop inside
these small pouches.

Sand

The sand beneath your feet on
the beach has been around for billions
of years, made from tiny pieces of
rock, the remains of creatures and
quartz minerals.

Leaves

Leaves are almost everywhere!
They tell us how plants make
oxygen. Look closely at their
tiny networks of tubes.

Tree resin

Tiny creatures today get stuck in
tree sap or resin just as ancient bugs,
lizards and frogs used to millions of
years ago. What old nature items
will you find stuck in sap?

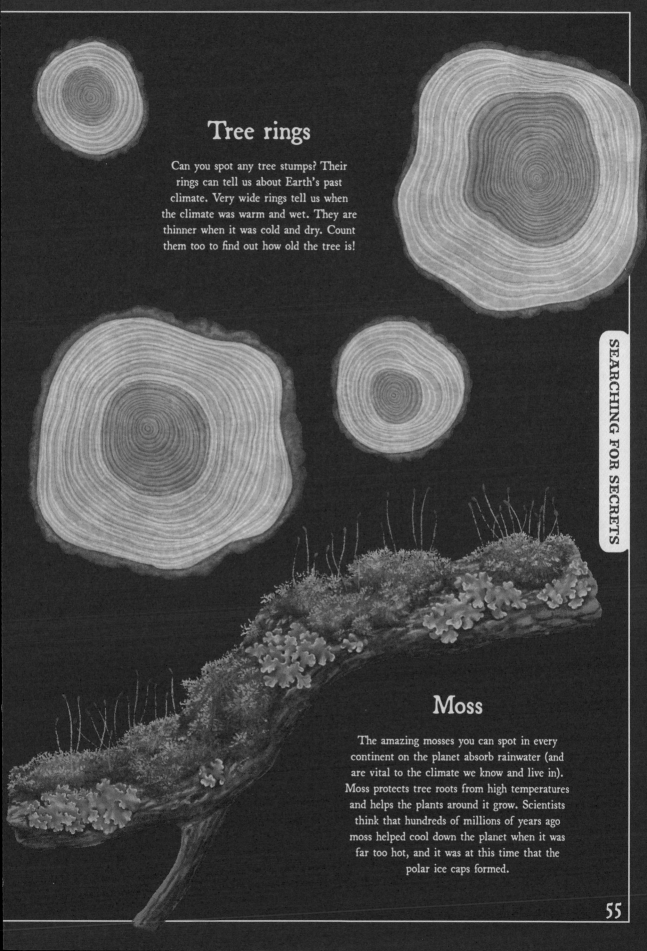

Tree rings

Can you spot any tree stumps? Their rings can tell us about Earth's past climate. Very wide rings tell us when the climate was warm and wet. They are thinner when it was cold and dry. Count them too to find out how old the tree is!

Moss

The amazing mosses you can spot in every continent on the planet absorb rainwater (and are vital to the climate we know and live in). Moss protects tree roots from high temperatures and helps the plants around it grow. Scientists think that hundreds of millions of years ago moss helped cool down the planet when it was far too hot, and it was at this time that the polar ice caps formed.

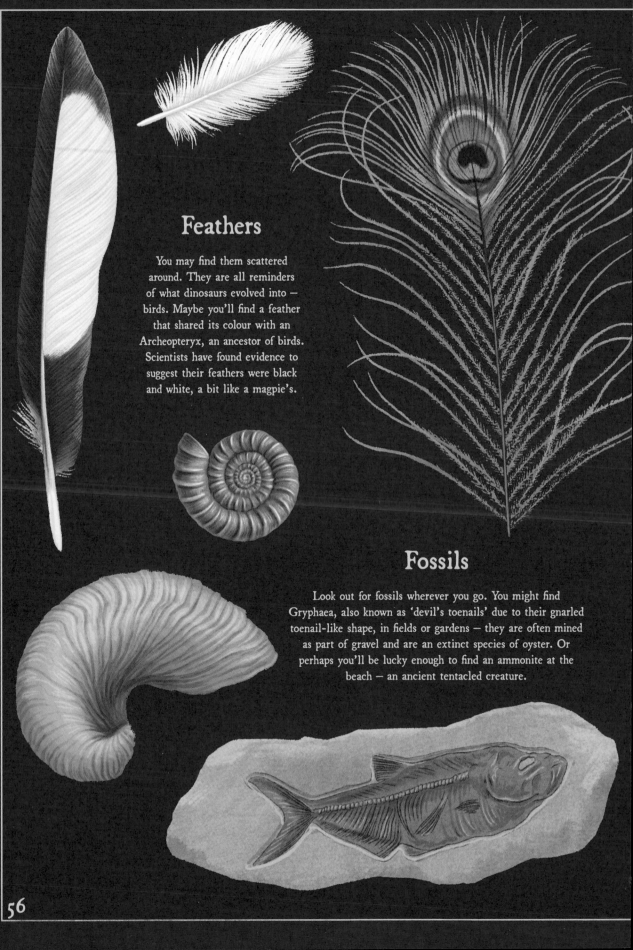

Feathers

You may find them scattered around. They are all reminders of what dinosaurs evolved into — birds. Maybe you'll find a feather that shared its colour with an Archeopteryx, an ancestor of birds. Scientists have found evidence to suggest their feathers were black and white, a bit like a magpie's.

Fossils

Look out for fossils wherever you go. You might find Gryphaea, also known as 'devil's toenails' due to their gnarled toenail-like shape, in fields or gardens — they are often mined as part of gravel and are an extinct species of oyster. Or perhaps you'll be lucky enough to find an ammonite at the beach — an ancient tentacled creature.

Seeds

Seeds come in all different shapes and sizes. A seed you find could be from a plant species that has been flowering, fruiting or generating seeds for millions of years, such as the magnolia plant.

Crystals

Some crystals are easier to find than others. Perhaps you'll find an old piece of quartz, a crystal that formed when magma cooled in the Earth's crust. We now know that some of the Earth's crust is made from quartz. And a lot of sandy beaches are made from tiny broken-down pieces of quartz.

FINDING EARTH'S SECRETS

For thousands of years, humans have been captivated by the natural world and have sought to uncover its secrets. We cannot know exactly what happened thousands, millions, or billions of years ago, but scientists use research, data and invention to piece stories of the past together. Each new discovery leads to another and helps shape our understanding of the world. Scientists use many clever methods to find and uncover Earth's secrets...

English naturalist Charles Darwin was the first person to publish a paper explaining the theory of evolution. Before this, most people could not have imagined that every living thing on Earth evolved from something else — something that often didn't look or act anything like its descendant! Darwin's research meant that now we knew we had common ancestors, we could try to piece together nature's family tree and how we came to be.

The discovery of elements also helped us to uncover some of Earth's secrets. There are currently 118 named elements that make up the Periodic Table, including carbon (an element that plants store and use to make oxygen). Scientists use what they know about elements to find out secrets of nature, such as how long ago something was alive on Earth. For example, scientists can use carbon dating to find out how old a fossil is. Plants store carbon. When animals eat plants or eat another animal that has eaten plant matter, they absorb the carbon too. When a living thing dies, it still stores carbon, which decreases over time. How much carbon is left in a fossil tells us how old it is. Carbon dating can tell us how old things are up to around 50,000 years. To help date something that is millions or billions of years old, scientists count the radioactive atoms found in the rock layer surrounding the fossil.

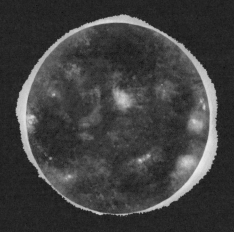

Scientists even use what they know about elements to tell us the stories of stars, including our closest star, the Sun. American astronomer Cecilia Payne-Gaposchkin helped discover that stars are mainly made from two elements, hydrogen and helium. We now know that once a star has burnt through its hydrogen, it sometimes explodes, starting the process of making new stars. Our galaxy was made from stars billions of years ago.

And scientists are discovering new things all the time, from faraway planets in outer space...

Over 5,000 new planets have been discovered to date.

...all the way back to the ground beneath our feet.

This new teeny-tiny-armed dinosaur was discovered in 2022. Scientists are piecing together the secrets of its past.

We still don't know for sure why a T-rex had such tiny arms or what the narwhal's long tooth is for, but nature's secret stories began 4.5 billion years ago and that is a lot of secrets to uncover. Hundreds, thousands, millions of years from now, many of the facts we think we know today will have changed and evolved with the development of new research and technology. So, for all the secret stories of nature in this book, it is not yet...

...THE END.

PROTECTING EARTH'S SECRETS

Earth and its secrets need protecting. Some creatures are in danger of becoming extinct because humans have been interfering with their habitat and contributing to climate change. Deforestation (when huge areas of forest are chopped down) destroys animals' habitats, meaning they lose both shelter and food. We all need to work together to replant trees, protect our oceans and combat climate change to protect the amazing stories of our wonderful planet.

These animals (and many others) are in danger, but we can help them and the creatures that live near our own homes, too...

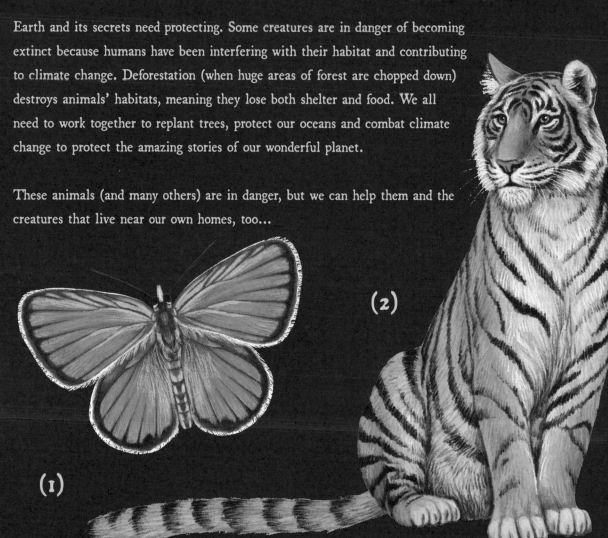

(1)

(2)

(1) Miami blue butterfly

Native to southern Florida in the US, this butterfly is one of the rarest insects in North America – the main threats to it are habitat loss, hurricanes and insecticides (chemicals that destroy insects). Humans can help lots of different butterfly species by creating wild areas in which they can feed and shelter. You can provide food for butterflies by planting flowering plants in your garden or in window boxes. You could research which butterfly species live near you and grow the kinds of plants those caterpillars and butterflies most like to feed on. Studying how insects and other animals behave helps us to protect them.

(2) Sunda tiger

Researchers think there are fewer than 400 Sunda tigers hiding in what is left of their forest in Sumatra, Indonesia. It has been cut down for oil palm and paper. Less forest means less prey for tigers, which means less food to eat. Tigers are hunted by poachers, too. Conservationists help them by planting trees and helping to look after their habitat. You can help all animals that live in forests by using recycled paper or paper that comes from forests that are being replanted. You could look for tissue products that are Forest Stewardship Council (FSC)-certified or 100% recycled.

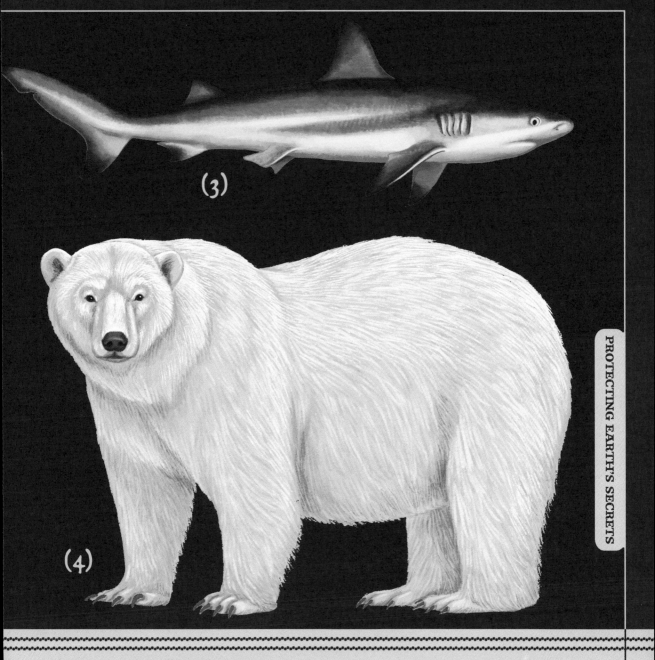

(3)

(4)

(3) Pondicherry shark

These sharks have become so rare, due to overfishing and loss of habitat, that they're hardly ever seen. But the Pondicherry shark is not the only endangered shark. Humans can help sharks by not hunting them and by protecting their ocean habitats. You can help too by asking your school to take part in National Shark Week. Most people are afraid of sharks — so by learning about them and telling others how amazing they are, we are helping people to respect them. Another way to help is by always remembering to keep beaches clean when we visit them because plastics and other rubbish can damage ocean habitats. You could also ask your parent or caregiver if you can take part in an official and safe beach clean-up.

(4) Polar bear

Climate change is the biggest reason that the polar bears' precious ice is melting. We can help polar bears and their icy world by battling climate change and burning less fuel. You can help by reducing how much electricity you use and what you throw away. For example, waste as little food as possible — a lot of energy goes into growing, collecting, cleaning and transporting food. The production of plastic and the throwing away of plastic contributes to climate change too, so you can also make sure that you buy food with less or no plastic packaging and always reuse plastic or recycle it where possible.

61

GLOSSARY

A

ANCESTOR – an early type of living thing from which other living things have developed and evolved

ANCIENT – very old

ASTEROID – a rocky object in space that goes around the Sun

B

BACTERIA – very tiny living things

BALEEN – fringed plates that baleen whales have instead of teeth to filter seawater for food such as krill

C

CAMOUFLAGE – the way an animal can use its appearance to blend in with its surroundings

CARBON DATING – a way of telling the age of a once-living thing by measuring the amount of carbon inside it

CARBON DIOXIDE

CARBON DIOXIDE – a gas made when things are burned and that living things, including humans, breathe out; very high levels of carbon dioxide are linked to global warming and climate change

CYLINDER – a long three-dimensional shape with a circle at each end

D

DESCENDANT – a living thing that is descended from a particular ancestor

E

ELEMENT – a substance that cannot be broken down into any simpler substance; elements are the building blocks for everything in the universe

EVOLVE – change over time

EXTINCT – no longer existing

F

FOSSIL – the remains or traces of living things from long ago

G

GRAVITY — an invisible force that pulls things together

H

HABITAT — the place where an animal or plant lives

HERBIVORE — an animal that eats plants

L

LICHEN — a dry-looking plant that grows on rocks, walls or trees

M

MARINE — to do with the sea

MASS EXTINCTION — the extinction of a large number of species in a relatively short period of time

MICROBE — a microscopic living thing, such as a bacterium, that can't be seen with the naked eye

MIGRATE — to move regularly from one place to another for food, space or breeding

O

ORGANISM — a living thing

P

POLLINATE — fertilise a plant so it can make seeds and new plants

POLYP — a tiny water animal with a tube-shaped body and tentacles around its mouth

PRIMATE — an animal of the group that includes humans, apes, lemurs and monkeys

Q

QUILL — the sharp spine of a porcupine or part of a feather

S

SOLAR SYSTEM — a star and the planets that move around it

SPECIES — a group of similar living things that can breed together

T

TETRAPOD — a four-footed animal

For George and Henry — S.G.

To Natasha and V — V.R.

Secret Stories of Nature © 2023 Quarto Publishing plc. Text © 2023 Saskia Gwinn
Illustrations © 2023 Vasilisa Romanenko.

First Published in 2023 by Wide Eyed Editions,
an imprint of The Quarto Group.
1 Triptych Place, London, SE1 9SH, United Kingdom.
T (0)20 7700 6700 F (0)20 7700 8066 **www.Quarto.com**

A catalogue record for this book is available from the British Library.

ISBN 978-0-71128-034-2

The illustrations were created digitally.
Set in Zapatista, Broadsheet and Trattarello.

Designer: Myrto Dimitrakoulia
Editors: Rachel Minay and Hannah Dove
Consultants: Sophie Stafford and Barbara Taylor
Production Controller: Dawn Cameron
Commissioning Editor: Claire Grace
Art Director: Karissa Santos
Publishers: Debbie Foy and Georgia Buckthorn

Manufactured in Guangdong, China TT072023

9 8 7 6 5 4 3 2 1

FSC
MIX
Paper | Supporting
responsible forestry
FSC® C016973
www.fsc.org